# THE BAHUTU MANIFESTO

# Note on the social aspect of the Indigenous racial issue in Rwanda

Published By

Suzeteo Enterprises

συζητεο πραγματων

***The Bahutu Manifesto:*** *Note on the Aocial Aspect of the Indigenous Racial Issue in Rwanda*

Edited by and with a foreword by Anthony Horvath, PhD.

Anthony Horvath is the Executive Director of Athanatos Christian Ministries.
www.athanatosministries.org

Translated by Hugo Zawada.

Hugo Zawada is a student, translator, and short story writer, based in Paris, France.

**ISBN: 978-1-947844-38-4**

Published by Suzeteo Enterprises, 2018.

Direct all requests and questions to publisher@suzeteo.com.

# Table of Contents

# Foreword

After World War II and the knowledge of what had transpired in Germany's concentrations camps had become well known, it was often said, "Never again!" The countries of the world vowed, more or less together, to never let a genocide occur again. Trials were held, conventions were agreed to, processes were established. The general feeling today, at least in the West, is that our world is far too civilized to allow something as horrific as the Holocaust occur again.

In modern minds, events that occurred 80 years ago or so, such as the Holocaust, may as well have occurred during the time of the Roman emperors. But those days of barbarism are behind us! But Rwanda's genocide occurred just 30 years ago. It happened in the living memory of most readers of this document.

Unlike my modern peers, I believe that civilization is a very thin veneer which can be punctured very easily in the right conditions. I am wary of any perspectives that maintain our barbarism is long gone. What happened in Rwanda in the mid-1990s is compelling evidence supporting my wariness.

I myself was just entering adulthood and have vague memories of the situation in Rwanda being reported on the news. To those who have studied what happened in Rwanda, they won't consider it a minor detail if I point out that I was always much more aware of what was going on in Bosnia than I was with what was happening in Rwanda, and to a lesser degree, Somalia.

But these instances support my wariness every bit as much as the Rwandan genocide does. The ugly truth is that if you just wait long enough, inevitably some group of people is going to massacre some other group of people. There is nothing in history to support any other viewpoint.

To the degree that it is possible to prevent or delay atrocities from actually occurring, it is necessary to go beyond "learning the lessons" these tragic events teach us, and learn the *right* lessons. In my opinion, humanity is still a long way off from learning the *right* lessons, which in itself is cause for concern.

One of the right lessons would be that we need to accept as real what I just said: "If you wait long enough, some group of people will massacre some other group." To put it another way, our experience of 'civilization' occurs in temporal and geographic pockets. *Today*, in *this* place, there is peace. But somewhere else, war is erupting. *Tomorrow* in *this* place, it is entirely possible that war might erupt, and in some other place, war is winding down, and peace is being established.

If you think of human evil as water slowly sloshing around a large pan, I think you will have the right idea. The reader may be standing in a dry spot in the pan today, but 10 years from now they may find themselves drowning, though they are standing in the very same place. Perhaps it will take longer than that—say, one or two hundred years—but the water *will* eventually reach and overwhelm that spot.

That being one of the *right* lessons, assuming we would like to mitigate the effects and impact of such events, it would be in our interest to study not just the trajedies, but also the successes. We need to know the factors that lead otherwise normal people to engage in mass murder, but also what factors are hedges against such behavior. But we should never fool ourselves into thinking that people 'today' are not capable of this or any other horrific behaviors.

Since, generally speaking, most people do find a way to get by without slaying their neighbor, it is not entirely a hopeless venture. The point I'm getting at here is that we should not consider peace as an accident, as though it was humanity's default state. If ever there was such a time that it was our default state, it is long gone! No. Peace is the aberration. Bloodshed is the historical norm. How do we keep peace? Firstly, we recognize that bloodshed is the historical norm, and also our *present* and *future* reality.

If you have found this document, it is possible that you are inclined to agree, so I won't belabor that point any further, but I emphasize it because it was the backdrop of my thinking when I set out to study the Rwandan genocide.

I discovered, in the course of that research, that there existed something called "The Bahutu Manifesto." This document apparently had some historical significance related to the genocide, but despite my efforts, I could not find a version of the Manifesto in English. Eventually, while scouring the Internet, I found what appears to be the original version, which was in French. I decided that I could simultaneously increase my own knowledge and contribute to the knowledge of others by commissioning a translation, which is what you hold in your hands now.

It is typical for the writers of forewords to put the contents of the book in a broader perspective. To tell you the truth, my ability to do that is limited. All of the sources that would help me situate the Manifesto properly in the context of the genocide are going to be in some other language, such as French, which I do not speak.

Thus, that is a task I will largely leave to others. There is one aspect that I am qualified to address, however, which every book I've read on the subject openly acknowledges was essential to the unfolding of the genocide. These sources make it absolutely clear that racism of a sort fueled the chaos, and they recognize that this racism was based on certain views on evolutionary theory held by the colonial powers, which was then imported to Rwanda, but rarely do you see these views called what they really are: *eugenics*.

Most people associate Germany's holocaust with the term 'eugenics.' However, it appears that Rwanda's genocide was also fueled by eugenic philosophies, only it took longer for the bitter fruit to manifest. There is another *right* lesson for us to absorb: just because a vicious ideology doesn't immediately result in murder or mayhem, it doesn't follow that it won't eventually do so.

Now, it is entirely possible that a book on the role of eugenics in fueling the Rwanda genocide exists. I just haven't found it yet. It may be in French, or some other language, and this could explain why I haven't seen it. As I don't know French, German, or Dutch—the three languages most likely to treat the topic, both pre-genocide and post-genocide—I am not able to properly situate the role of eugenic thinking in the history of Rwanda. That, too, will have to be someone else's job.

What I can do, however, is offer some broad remarks on it as it relates to this very document, which I will do so briefly.

Eugenics is something that I know a bit about: my doctoral dissertation was on Darwinism and eugenics, and I am the owner and administrator of the website eugenics.us, which is, as it were, a repository for my research. As I have time, energy, and resources, I have been publishing as much primary source material to this website as I can.

While most people openly renounce eugenics these days,

they do not renounce the optimism that the eugenicists had. Among many of the other things that the eugenicists believed was the idea that human society could be perfected by the application of science. Indeed, the feeling was that if one knew something to be empirically true, one had a veritable obligation to apply it. This attitude, that just because something is 'evidence based' it follows you *ought* to act on it, is alive and well, I assure you!

### Rwanda's Identity Cards

When the Germans arrived in Rwanda around 1890, they brought with them their viewpoints on evolutionary differences between human populations. The term 'eugenics' had only just been coined by Galton in 1883, so you won't find it very often, if at all, in the German writings of the time, although a researcher might find more under the phrase, *rassenhygiene*, although even this term was not coined until 1895 by the German biologist, Alfred Ploetz.

I trust I do not have to explain to the reader that the Germans took their theories on race *very* seriously. In Rwanda, then Germans probably found further proof of their views. They quickly identified the Tutsi as being a more advanced subset of the human species—because they appeared more European, and of course, the Europeans were (naturally) at the top of the human evolutionary chart. The Hutus stood out to the Germans as being obviously inferior.

Thus, the Germans treated the Tutsis more favorably than they treated the Hutus. More importantly, for our purposes, they transmitted this viewpoint on race and evolution to the native Rwandans, who—even more importantly—seemed to accept it as genuine fact.

The German influence on Rwanda was relatively short-lived. After World War I, the Germans lost their claim on

Rwanda to the Belgians. It may surprise the reader to discover that the Belgians saw Rwanda just as the Germans had. That's because the Belgians took *their* theories on race *very* seriously, as well.

This is a little known fact, obscured in large part because Germany's actions on eugenic lines were so massive that they made the eugenic viewpoints of other nations seem small in comparison. However, eugenics viewpoints were pervasive in almost every nation of the world at the time, including England, France, the United States, Japan, and yes, Belgium. Why? Because it was SCIENCE! That's why.

In actuality, eugenics philosophies fueled the murders of hundreds of thousands, if not millions, of people, around the world beyond what transpired in Germany. The Rwandan genocide, in its own way, added a million all by itself.

The Belgians continued to show favoritism to the Tutsis, and Hutus and Tutsis alike continued to accept the judgement of 'science' on them—if not the idea that one was biologically superior to the other, at least the idea that they were at least biologically distinct.

This persisted until after World War II, when something peculiar happened: it was no longer seemly to apply Darwinism to human populations. Like a meteor hurtling to the ground, eugenics fell out of favor almost overnight. If you suppose that this had something to do with what was discovered to have happened in Germany, you would be supposing correctly.

As explicit eugenic thinking faded rapidly from public favor, principles of democracy were given heightened emphasis. In Rwanda, this resulted in an astonishing change in fortunes for the Hutus. They were in the majority in Rwanda and were now elevated by the Belgians. The

Tutsus, being in minority, lost their favored treatment. It appears that the Belgians did not merely withdraw their support for the Tutsis, but actively undermined them at the expense of the Hutus. This did not go over well.

Within a period of twenty years, the place of the Hutus and the Tutsis had almost completely reversed, but the racial boundaries were retained. The Bahutu Manifesto is a snapshot of Hutu views near the end of this reversal. As you read it, you will see that the Hutus obviously welcomed Belgium's new posture towards them, albeit with some skepticism, but also that the racial distinctions brought by the colonial powers not only persisted, but were accepted as reality by Rwandans.

To what degree this acceptance of racial principles, as *scientifically established fact*, would lead to the actual genocide forty years later, is beyond what I am qualified to address. That *race* as a controlling factor in Rwandan polity would persist is, however, obvious and undeniable, and the Manifesto provides insight into this reality.

In the Bahutu Manifesto, we have a vivid example of how pernicious ideologies can bear their fruit even after generations have gone by, in ways that were perhaps impossible to foresee, and seem surprising even in retrospect. I am speaking of the Hutu decision in the late 1950s, as reflected in this paragraph from pages 23-24, to retain the identity cards which recorded whether or not someone was a Hutu or a Tutsi:

> Moreover, people have taken notice of the indirect administration's support of the MuTutsi monopoly. In order to better watch over this racial monopoly, we vigorously oppose – at least for now – the removal of the

"MuHutu", "MuTutsi", "MuTwa" mentions in official identification documents. Their removal is likely to further promote the selection by veiling it and preventing statistics from containing factual data.

While the sentiments driving the genocide would almost certainly have existed without the identification cards reflecting which 'race' a person belonged to, it is widely agreed that it was the identification cards that made mass scale targeting of the Tutsis possible on a practical level.

The Hutu authors of the Bahutu Manifesto were keen to continue identifying themselves and others according to whether or not they were Hutu or Tutsis in order to make sure, *objectively*, that Tutsis were no longer receiving favored treatment. This decision would prove fatal, some forty years later, to nearly a million Rwandans.

There obviously were many factors that lead to the genocide. The many arrogances of colonialism were expressed dramatically in Rwanda. The failure of the Roman Catholic church to live according to its transcendental values was catastrophic. The absence of the international community when it counted most is shocking. Still, when it came right down to it, what mattered most at the roadblock was what race it said you were on your identity card.

It hurts one's head to contemplate that something as inoccuous as an identity card listing one's race could be used to slaughter your grandchildren long after you are dead, but there it is.

## Conclusion

It would be nice if we could chalk up humanity's atrocities to one form or another of racism. Unfortunately, it is clear from history that humans have relied on a wide variety of pretexts for killing each other. Nonetheless, the acceptance of Darwinism and, by extension, the acceptance of the idea that we ought to apply Darwinism (and it is *a scientific fact*, so why *wouldn't* we apply it?), can be linked to the murders of millions of people in the 20th century.

It is conceivable that it can be linked to the murders of millions of people in the 21st century, which is still unfolding. With the lineage that it has, one may hope that we can recognize how it twists its way through human societies, and perhaps mitigate its effects.

Well, a man can hope.

If the *right* lessons are drawn, maybe we'll even have good reason to hope. Otherwise, not so much.

Dr. Anthony Horvath
Executive Director of Athanatos Christian Ministries

February, 2018.

## A note on this edition:

The translator was directed to, in the main, go for a literal translation. However, in some cases it seemed necessary to convey the idea rather than the words, in order to understand what the authors were trying to communicate. The original French edition that this English translation is based on is included at the end. This will allow people to investigate nuances of the text, themselves. Apart from this, the only change to the text concerns the outlining: Where confusion was likely to arise, subpoints 1, 2, 3, etc, were changed to subpoints A, B, and C, etc.

# THE BAHUTU MANIFESTO

## Note on the Social Aspect of the Indigenous Racial Issue in Rwanda

### March 24th, 1957

Rumours will have already reached the Government's authority, through the press or perhaps also by word-of-mouth about the current situation regarding MuHutu-MuTutsi relations in Rwanda. Unconscious or not, they highlight a problem that we find important, an issue which could mar and one day possibly torpedo the incredible work that Belgium has been carrying out. The Indigenous racial issue certainly comes from within, but hardly anything ever remains local in this day and age!

How can it stay concealed just when Indigenous and Europeans political complications seem to be clashing? In addition to political, social and economical complications, the element of race has provoked greater and greater animosity. Indeed, through culture, the advantages of modern civilisation clearly appear to be leaning towards one side, – the MuTutsi side – laying out more hardship in the future than what we commonly call "dividing issues" today. It would indeed serve no lasting purpose to resolve the

Belgo-MuTutsi problem if the fundamental MuHutu-MuTutsi issue is left behind.

It is to this issue we wish to participate and bring certain clarifications. We have deemed it constructive to show its frightening realities in a few words to the Guardianship Authority, which exists for the entire population rather than an elite representing a mere 14% of inhabitants.

The current situation underlines an important imbalance created by Rwanda's former socio-political structure, particularly the *ubuhake*, and by the intensive and generalised application of the indirect administration, as well as by the vanishing of certain ancient social institutions which have been erased without allowing corresponding modern, western institutions to take their place. We would also be pleased to see trade unionism be implemented shortly, to help and encourage the emergence of a strong middle class. Fear, inferiority complex and the atavistic need for a tutor, associated to the essence of the MuHutu, if real, are the after-effect of the feudal system. Supposing their reality implies that the civilisation brought by the Belgian would only have been useful had they made positive efforts to lift those obstacles for the full emancipation of Rwanda.

# 1.
# FALSE OBJECTIONS AGAINST THE ASCENT OF MUHUTU

Against the rise of the MuHutu, numerous objections are presented. Without ignoring the shortcomings of the MuHutu, as it is our belief that every race and class has their own shortcomings, we would like to see action be taken to correct them rather than systematically suppress the BaHutu into an eternally inferior situation. The particular claims are the following:

a) "That the BaHutu were once leaders of the country". A subtle anachronism that cannot be adequately confirmed today.

b) The social virtues of the MuTutsi would present it as *"natus ad imperium"*[1]! The same virtue can be presented just as well by the Italian than the German, by the English than the Japanese, by the Flemish than the Walloon.

c) "What have the advanced BaHutu done for the ascension of their peers?" – It is a matter of atmosphere, and

---

[1] 'born to rule.'

especially of the *ubuhake*, which has often influenced the nomination system. Next, the lack of necessary freedom of initiative in an absolutist structure, the economical inferiority imposed on the MuHutu by social structures, and the constantly menial jobs they are given handicap all attempts of the MuHutu for their peers.

d) "For heaven's sake, they should either present their applications, or wait for the inferiority complex to be over" – Applications imply a certain democratic dimension, or one would have to ignore what this claim suggests about its leanings regarding the *ubuhake* tradition that people have abandoned (without actually abandoning respect towards authority). Regarding that matter, let us recall the reflection of a noteworthy Hamite: "The BaHutu should not be raised by the white man, but by the traditional MuTutsi!" We do not believe the ancient ennobling to be a practise worth resuscitating in the Afro-European meeting.

e) "And the masses will follow" – The elite-mass interaction is undeniable, provided that the elite is the mass. In essence, the issue stems from colonialism on two levels: The MuHutu having to bear the Hamite and his domination, and the European's laws systematically having to pass through the MuTutsi (*leta mbirigi* and *leta nTutsi*)! The "White-Hamite-MuHutu" chain method should be ruled out. Numerous examples have shown that "the masses" do not always automatically follow.

f) "Union, as a prerequisite for the unique and common front in favour of the country's independence, must silence the BaHutu demands." – It is highly disputable that a union of this kind, in other words a single-party, would really be necessary if emancipation is already a ripe fruit! – Furthermore, the section of the population that the European departure could reduce to an even worse servitude would at the very least have the right to refuse cooperating towards the independence, by other means than through hard work and the demonstration of the deficiencies that it would deem necessary to correct first.

# 2.
# WHAT IS THE INDIGENOUS RACIAL ISSUE?

Some have wondered whether it is a question of social conflict, or one of racial conflict. We believe this to be of trifling importance. In the reality of things and in the minds of people, it is a question of both. We could however specify: the problem is above all else a problem of political monopoly owned by one race, the MuTutsi. A political monopoly which given the current structures, also becomes an economical and social monopoly. This political, economical and social monopoly, given the *de facto* selections in education, manages to become even a cultural monopoly, much to the BaHutu's despair, who see themselves as doomed to remain eternal menial labourers, and on top of that, after a potential independence they will have helped conquer without knowing what they are doing. The *ubuhake* may have been removed, but it is has been replaced by this total monopoly which, for the most part, causes the abuses which the population has been complaining about.

*Political monopoly.* – The so-called ancient BaHutu chiefs were only exceptions that prove the rule! And the opportunities which allowed those exceptions in the first place have ceased to exist: re-establishing the old BaHutu ennoblement is obviously out of question. As for the infamous inter-breeding or "mutations" from BaHutu to Hamites, only statistics, well established genealogy, and perhaps also doctors can give us accurate information that is objective and solid enough to refute the common sense to which we yet refer for numerous other things.

*Economical and social monopoly.* – The privileges of his brother who commands the hill have always contributed to raise the private MuTutsi. Certain social functions were even "reserved" to nobility, and through the indirect administration, current civilisation has only reinforced if not almost generalised this privilege. The recent sharing of cows has clearly demonstrated the shortcomings of property at least when it comes to livestock. The land itself in over half of Rwanda – The most Hamitised regions – is barely a true property for the occupant. This in fact unstable occupation does not incentivise labour and as a consequence, it handicaps people with only their arms to make their money. We remain silent about the system of all kinds of forced labour, the MuHutu's only monopoly, leaving the MuTutsi with a head start to promote the finances of his house.

*Cultural monopoly* – Once more we could question the traits of real Hamites in a few numbers; but the *de facto* (coincidentally?) currently presented by secondary establishments makes it blatant. There are more than enough arguments to demonstrate that the MuHutu is inapt, that he is poor, that he does not know how to behave. Inaptitude remains to be proven; poverty is only the consequence of the current social system; as for manners, we suggest a greater open-mindedness. Tomorrow diplomas will be asked for, and it will be considered fair, and diplomas are generally only from one side, the MuHutu doesn't even know what this word means. And if by coincidence (God forbid) another force were to intervene, which would oppose great numbers, bitterness and despair to the diplomas, the racial element would complicate everything and there will be no point in wondering wether it is a racial or social conflict.

We believe this total monopoly to be at the root of all the abuses which the populations have been complaining about.

A few relevant facts and currents can depict the true state of things today:

1. The MuHutu youth (A few completely fallen BaTutsi individuals suffer the same fate) which has for their motto, *"In itineribus semper"*[2] inside and outside the country, flees forced labour, is no longer adapted to the State and to today's psychology, and rejects or barely accepts the scourge of obligation, which incidentally provides an opportunity for the abuses that the authorities seem to be unaware of.

2. Fathers who barely provide for their families; in politics, a sort of propaganda, possibly unconsciously, pushes them to antipathy towards the European; a hefty number of them believe that the Belgian Government is linked to nobility in favour of their complete exploitation.

---

[2] 'always on the roads'

3. On the other hand however, thoughts such as this are still very common: "Without the European, we would be doomed to an even more inhumane exploitation than in the past, to total destruction. It is regrettable even that the European isn't the one to become leader, deputy, or judge", not that they believe the European to be perfect, but because he is the lesser of two evils. The passive resistance of deputies across several levels is only the consequence of this instability and of this uneasiness.

4. The regret of the BaHutu to witness their people almost systematically brought down to menial positions. Every policy involved in this repression now fools only a few. All of this is only one step away from a "cold" civil war and xenophobia.

# 3.
# PROPOSAL OF IMMEDIATE SOLUTIONS

A few solutions can be brought up, effective only if the current political and social system changes deeply and quickly.

**1. *The first solution is a "mindset".*** – Let us give up the idea that the Rwandan elites are only present within the Hamites (an idea cherished by the administration of our country and which we commonly call "Umuco w'Igihugu", "the respect of national culture and customs").

**2. *From social and economical points of view.*** – We wish to see the creation of institutions helping the MuHutu population. The latter has been handicapped by an indigenous administration, which appears to want the MuHutu to remain in poverty, and therefore in the impossibility to claim effective exercise of his rights, in his own country. We suggest:

A. *The deletion of forced labour.* – Forced labourers would be replaced by a public works service (public or parastatal) that hires truly voluntary workers, who would be defended by social legislation, which has made great recent progress. This service could be conceived and realised like the Regideso, as far as we know it. The deletion of forced labour would give populations the little freedom necessary to undertake useful initiatives. The indolent – which also exist among casts of elites – would be watched over by a more humane system.

B. *Legal recognition of individual land property* in the Western meaning of the word. Everyone would have an area sufficient for crops and livestock, and the bikingi (pasture) of the bourgeoisie would be removed, at least in the way customs see and protect it. For this legislation, a competent service should determine the amount of land needed to feed a family of 6-8 children, given the productive capabilities of Rwanda-Urundi soil. All those who currently own this land of this surface would be registered by the sous-chefferies as true proprietors in the Western sense; and the rest would gradually follow, supported by the movement of displacement that has begun in certain regions of the country.

Regarding land property, measures should not be taken too quickly, even under the proposal of the National Council, in which many members would be tempted to see the problem in a one-sided way, or without accounting for the hardships and concrete aspirations of the commoner.

C. *A rural credit fund.* – Its main objective would be to promote rural initiative: rational agriculture and various professions. This fund would lend to the peasant who wants to set himself up as a farmer or an artisan. The access conditions to this fund should however be accessible to the ordinary MuHutu.

D. *The economical union of Belgian Africa and the mainland.* – This union should take place under norms to be specified and suggested first to the public and those in charge before being recognised.

E. *Freedom of expression.* – There have been talks about the dissolving effects of a certain local press, indigenous, European, or even metropolitan, which tends to divide the races. We believe that certain exaggerations may have taken place, like in any piece of journalism, especially considering the age of the regarded countries. We also think that certain expressions may have offended some people who are not used to being upset, and who yet do what they please with the small and the weak. This may have collided with a system barely which has barely come out of feudalism. It is also our belief that freedom of expression in Belgian Africa and regarding concrete issues concerning populations that aren't older than three years, certain authorities that aren't used to democracy, and who perhaps do not wish for it, have been upset. But we also think that one shouldn't use the pretext of not wanting a "divide" to hush situations that exist or tend to exist to the detriment of a great number of people, and for the monopoly of an abusive minority. We are convinced that neither Belgian

Justice nor the Belgian Government would accept a union carried out on the corpses of a population who wishes for necessary conditions and atmosphere to better work and develop. Before demanding perfection from the press, shouldn't one demand it from the indigenous courts, from the administration, which are far more important and provide far too many opportunities for press critics? Isn't well intended freedom of expression one of the foundations for true democratisation?

**3. *From a political point of view.*** – Even though we agree that the current MuTutsi administration contributes more and more to the country's government, we however wish to warn against a method that while tending towards the suppression of black-white colonialism, would promote a worse type of colonialism of the Hamite over the MuHutu. It is necessary to iron out the difficulties that may arise from the Hamite monopoly onto the other races that have lived longer and in bigger number in this country. We wish for this purpose:

A. For laws and customs to be codified. It is certain that there are some customs that we cannot erase with the stroke of a pen, but we believe that the almost superstitious praise of the cherished "custom" handicaps the entire and solid progress made by the populations. In addition, for more clarity, legal equality, and for less confusion and abuse: we demand that the laws carried by Belgian authority and the customs that remain useful, reasonable and not impervious to the country's democratisation be listed in a Code that could regularly be revised and modified depending on the degree of evolution. The works of scholars and legislators on those matters facilitate the speed of this urgent task. Indigenous and European courts and administration, the rise of private initiative in all domains, are both in need of such a guide. The brandishing of the sword that is the country's custom (*umuco w'igihugu*) by monopolistic interests is not likely to promote the necessary confidence, nor to establish justice and peace facing the current aspirations of the people. It is necessary to list and codify in order to realise the real deficiencies and correct them, so as to further promote private initiative that often struggles against absolutisms or local interpretations stripped of any social sense.

B. For the BaHutu to be effectively promoted to civil service (chefferie,[3] sous-chefferies, judges). And concretely we believe that it is time for those respective councils or the ratepayers to now elect their chefs, sous-chefs and judges. In certain outdated localities, the authority could suggest two or three candidates among which they would choose their leader.

C. For indigenous civil services to have a certain duration, after which people could elect someone else, or re-elect the same person if they have proven satisfactory. Such a system, without being racist, would give the MuHutu more chances and would get back at the abuse of a life long monopoly.

---

[3] *Chefferie* is the official term to refer to the different districts in Rwanda, each appointed with their Chef (or leader) which was very often a MuHutu. Likewise, sous-chefferies represent the different subdistricts.

D. For province leaders to be removed from chefferie councils.

E. For the composition of the superior council of the country to be made through deputation by the chefferies: each chefferie would delegate a number proportional to that of its ratepayers, without excluding the Europeans, who will be permanently housed inside the chefferie. We do not see it as naïve to accept the Europeans, permanently set in the district; it is that if they set that way, they have definitive interest in defending it; it is that the legislation must be expanded more and more, and be less discriminatory, and that the Europeans are at least just as useful as a MuTutsi in the region.

Measures such as the ones we suggest seem essential to us, if the government wants to build a something with a future and without favouritism. We can understand the need for caution but we believe that the experience of nine hundred years of Tutsi domination and 56 years of European tutelage is more than enough, and that waiting is likely to compromise all that we are building.

**4.** *From an educational point of view.* – Tomorrow diplomas will be asked for, and it will be fair. But up until now the *de facto* selection at secondary and post secondary education has been blatant. The excuses are plenty, and some are not without reason: they take advantage of a system that systematically favours the political and economical advancement of the Hamite.

A. We want education to be under close watch. It is necessary to be more realistic and modern by giving up the *de facto* selection whose results can be witnessed in secondary education. This needs to be done in the early years, so that one doesn't have to chose from the few BaTutsi in the fifth year. There may not be a positive drive in the selection, but the *de facto* is much more significant and often caused by the chain system that we have mentioned earlier. In order to avoid *de facto* selection, *caeteris aequalibus*[4]; if there aren't enough spots, we would pertain to the birth certificates in order to respect the proportions. Not that we should spiral into the

---

[4] 'others are equal'

opposite direction and Bantuise where we have Hamitised. Current social standings should in no way influence admission into schools.

B. We want the gifting of scholarships (a part of which comes from the taxes of the population, predominantly MuHutu) to be monitored by the tutelary government, so that the BaHutu cease to be a springboard for the unbearable monopoly that holds them forever inferior socially and politically.

C. As for higher education, we believe that the institutions located in Belgian Africa are enough, but should accept as many students as possible, without however opposing individuals – very capable, and specialised – who study in metropolitan universities.

As for university in Rwanda, it is necessary not to waste the so called deficit budget and focus first one building vocational and technical education, which the country has barely any of, while this type of education is at the core of economical emancipation. It is not simply about constantly blocking the entry to European universities for handpicked candidates who consider specialisations that are actually directly useful to the country.

D. We want artisanal, vocational, and professional education, for the coming phase, to be the budget's first priority. This education needs to be generalised as quickly as possible. This education however, needs to be as cheap as possible to for the sons of the people to access. We have indeed noticed that the few attempts at artisanal installations appear destined to host the overflow of the MuTutsi youth who do not have the capabilities, or simply cannot find a spot to get into secondary education.

We wish that shortly, and while we implementat the professional and technical equipment, each chefferies be equipped with an elementary Centre for Rural Education of at least two years, where primary teaching is extended (and applied to life) and above all where children who cannot access secondary education receive manual training. It is for us, from the educational perspective, the main and immediate objective we will assign the C.A.C.s to, which are all in all fed by taxes, largely from the MuHutu. The money spent on the Biru (tambourine drummers of the courts) and on the Dances which are normally recruited by nobility contradicts the claim that "money is an issue".

E. We want social welfare homes to be established and multiplied for the attention of young women and young girls from rural environments, who with reduced finances, cannot access the aristocratic housekeeping or instructing schools. The balance of domestic evolution of the country demands the generalisation of this basic education.

*In summary*, we wish for the complete and collective promotion of the MuHutu; those interested are already working on it, during the short free time that their labour allows. We also demand action be taken from above, more positive and resolute. Belgium has done a lot in that sense, we must admit, but its humanity must not stop now. It is not that we want things to falter: we agree that the Tutsi superior council could contribute progressively and more effectively to the country's affairs; but stronger still, we demand from the tutelary government and Tutsi administration that a more positive and productive action be taken for the political and economical emancipation of the traditional Hamite.

Overall, we ask from Belgium to give up on forcing the MuHutu to constantly hop in the tow of the MuTutsi. We ask that in social relations, for example, we abandon the custom of requiring (tacitly, of course) the MuHutu to behave like the MuTutsi in order to be considered "acceptable". Because we claim to respect cultures, it also important to take into account the differences in Rwandan culture. The Hamite's customs may be appealing to some, but we haven't yet agreed that all the other blacks should first go through hamitisation in order to learn from the Westerner and access civilisation. It is hard to prove the necessity to have the MuHutu in the Hamite's tow, the need for the constant intervention of this political, social, economical and cultural tow.

Moreover, people have taken notice of the indirect administration's support of the MuTutsi monopoly. In order to better watch over this racial monopoly, we vigorously oppose – at least for now – the removal of the "MuHutu", "MuTutsi", "MuTwa" mentions in official identification documents. Their removal is likely to further promote the selection by veiling it and preventing statistics from containing factual data. No one said that it was the name that bothered the MuHutu; it is rather the privileges of a favoured monopoly, which runs the risk of reducing the majority of the population to systematic inferiority and undeserved sub-standard existence.

It is a constructive drive and a wholesome desire to collaborate that have pushed us to shed an additional light onto an issue so important to the eyes of those who genuinely love this country; an issue in which the tutelary responsibilities of Belgium are all too involved. It is not at all as revolutionaries (in the negative sense of the word) but as partners, conscious of our social duty, that we are committed to warn the authorities against the dangers that could stem sooner or later from the preservation of a racist monopoly in Rwanda. A few voices of the people have already reported this anomaly; passive resistance, still awaiting the intervention of the White tutor, is likely to intensify, when faced with the abuse of a monopoly that is no longer tolerated; this is already a sign.

Authorities will want in this short note the somewhat systematised flow of ideas and concrete desires of the people, which we are a part of, with which we share life and the repressions operated by an atmosphere which tends to obstruct the true democratisation of the country. This democratisation generously proposed by Belgium is deeply demanded by the population, avid for a viable and favourable socio-political atmosphere, conductive to initiative and effort towards betterment, and the total and collective promotion of the people.

SIGNED:

Maximilien NIYONZIMA

Godefroid SENTAMA

Grégoire KAYBANDA

Silvestre MUNYAMBONERA

Claver NDAHAYO

Joseph SIBOMANA

Isidore NZEYIMANA

Joseph HABYARIMANA

Calliopé MULINDAHABI

# Manifeste des Bahutu

Note sur l'aspect social du problème racial indigène au Ruanda

24 mars 1957

Des rumeurs sont déjà parvenues à l'autorité du Gouvernement par la presse et peut-être aussi par la parole au sujet de la situation actuelle des relations muhutu-mututsi au Ruanda. Inconscientes ou non, elles touchent un problème qui nous paraît grave, problème qui pourrait déparer ou peut-être même un jour torpiller l'oeuvre si grandiose que la Belgique réalise au Ruanda. Le problème racial indigène est sans doute d'ordre intérieur, mais qu'est-ce qui reste intérieur ou local à l'âge où le monde en arrive!

Comment peut-il rester caché au moment où les complications politiques indigènes et européennes semblent s'affronter? Aux complications politiques, sociales et économiques s'ajoute l'élément race dont l'aigreur semble s'accentuer de plus en plus. En effet, par le canal de la culture, les avantages de la civilisation actuelle semblent se diriger carrément d'un côté, - le côté mututsi - préparant ainsi plus de difficultés dans l'avenir que ce qu'on se plaît à appeler aujourd'hui "les problèmes qui divisent". Il ne servirait en effet à rien de durable de solutionner le problème mututsi-belge si l'on laisse le problème fondamental mututsi-muhutu.

C'est à ce problème que nous voulons contribuer à apporter quelques éclaircissements. Il nous a paru constructif d'en montrer en quelques mots les réalités angoissantes à l'Autorité Tutélaire qui est ici pour toute la population et non pour une caste qui représente à peine 14 % des habitants.

La situation actuelle présente un grand déséquilibre qui est créé par l'ancienne structure politico-sociale du Ruanda, en particulier le buhake, et de l'application à fond et généralisé de l'administration indirecte, ainsi que par la disparition de certaines institutions sociales anciennes qui ont été effacées sans qu'on ait permis à ces institutions modernes, occidentales correspondantes de s'établir et de compenser. Aussi serions-nous heureux de voir s'établir rapidement le syndicalisme aider et encourager la formation d'une classe moyenne forte. La peur, le complexe d'infériorité et le besoin "atavique" d'un tuteur, attribués à l'essence du Muhutu, si tant est vrai qu'ils sont une réalité, sont des séquelles du système féodal. A supposer leur réalité, la civilisation qu'apportent les Belges n'aurait réalisé grand'chose, s'il n'était fait des efforts positifs pour lever effectivement ces obstacles à l'émancipation du Ruanda intégral.

## I. - Objections prétextées contre la promotion du muhutu

Contre l'ascension du Muhutu, nombreuses sont les objections qu'on présente. Sans ignorer les déficiences du Muhutu, nous pensons que chaque race et chaque classe a les siennes et nous voudrions une action qui les corrige au lieu de refouler systématiquement les Bahutu dans une situation éternellement inférieure. On présente spécialement:

a) "Que les Bahutu furent chefs dans le pays." - Anachronisme raffiné que le présent ne peut confirmer suffisamment.

b) "Les vertus sociales du Mututsi qui le présenteraient comme natus ad imperium!" - La même vertu peut être présentée autrement par un Italien que par un Allemand, par un Anglais que par un Japonais, par un Flamand que par un Wallon.

c) "Qu'ont fait les Bahutu évolués pour l'ascension de leurs congénaires?" - C'est une question d'atmosphère et du buhake particulièrement qui a souvent influencé le système des nominations. Ensuite le manque de liberté suffisante à l'initiative dans une structure absolutiste, l'infériorité économique imposée au Muhutu par les structures sociales, les fonctions systématiquement subalternes où ils sont tenus, handicapent tout essai du Muhutu pour ses congénaires.

d) "Que diable ils présentent leurs candidatures ou prétendent que le complexe d'infériorité soit liquidé". - Les candidatures supposent un sens démocratique, ou alors il faut honorer ce que ce prétexte peut laisser entendre de tendance au buhake que les gens ont abandonné (sans pour autant abandonner le respect de l'autorité).

A ce sujet, il faudrait rappeler la réflexion d'un hamite notable: "Il ne faudrait pas que les Bahutu soient élevés par les soins du blanc, mais par la méthode traditionnelle du Mututsi!" Nous ne pensons pas que l'ancien ennoblissement soit une pratique à ressusciter dans la rencontre Europe-Afrique.

e) "Et les foules suivront." - L'interaction élite-masse est indéniable, mais à condition que l'élite soit de la masse. Au fond du problème il s'agit d'un colonialisme à deux étages: le Muhutu devant supporter le hamite et sa domination et l'Européen et ses lois passant systématiquement par le canal du mututsi (leta mbirigi et leta ntutsi)! La méthode de la remorque "blanc-hamite-muhutu" est à exclure. Des exemples ont pu montrer que "les foules" ne suivent pas automatiquement toujours.

f) "L'union, condition de front commun et unique pour l'indépendance du pays, doit faire taire toutes les revendications bahutu." - Il est fort douteux que l'union de cette manière, le parti unique, soit vraiment nécessaire si en fait l'émancipation est fruit mûr! - Ajoutons que la section de la population que le départ de l'Européen pourrait réduire dans une servitude pire que la première, aurait tout au moins le droit de s'abstenir de coopérer à l'indépendance autrement que par des efforts de travail acharné et de manifestations des déficiences qu'il lui semble nécessaire de soigner d'abord.

## II. - En quoi consiste le problème racial indigène?

D'aucuns se sont demandés s'il s'agit là d'un conflit social ou d'un conflit racial. Nous pensons que c'est de la littérature. Dans la réalité des choses et dans les réflexions des gens, il est l'un et l'autre. On pourrait cependant préciser: le problème est avant tout un problème de monopole politique dont dispose une race, le mututsi: monopole politique qui, étant donné l'ensemble des structures actuelles, devient un monopole économique et social; monopole politique, économique et social qui, vu les sélections *de facto* dans l'Enseignement, parvient à être un monopole culturel, au grand désespoir des Bahutu qui se voient condamnés à rester d'éternels manoeuvres subalternes, et pis encore, après une indépendance éventuelle qu'ils auront aidé à conquérir sans savoir ce qu'ils font. Le buhake est sans doute supprimé, mais il est mieux remplacé par ce monopole total qui, en grande partie, occasionne les abus dont la population se plaint.

- Monopole politique.- Les prétendus anciens chefs bahutu

ne furent que des exceptions, pour confirmer la règle! Et les occasions qui permettaient ces exceptions n'existent plus: il ne s'agit évidemment pas de rétablir la vieille coutume de l'ennoblissement des Bahutu. Quant aux fameux métissages ou "mutations" de bahutu en hamites, la statistique, une généalogie bien établie et peut-être aussi les médecins, peuvent seuls donner des précisions objectives et assez solides pour réfuter le sens commun auquel on se réfère pourtant pour bien d'autres choses.

- Monopole économique et social.- Les privilèges de son frère qui commande la colline ont toujours concouru à rehausser le Mututsi privé. Certaines fonctions sociales furent même "réservées" à la noblesse et la civilisation actuelle, par l'administration indirecte, n'a fait que renforcer et quasi généraliser cette réserve. Le récent partage des vaches a bien montré la faiblesse de la propriété en fait de bétail en moins. La terre elle-même dans plus de la moitié du Ruanda - les régions les plus hamitisées - est à peine une vraie propriété pour l'occupant. Cette occupation en fait précaire n'encourage guère le travail et en conséquence les gens qui n'ont que leurs bras pour s'enrichir en sont désavantagés. Nous laissons sous silence le système de tous genres de corvées, seul monopole du Muhutu, le Mututsi ayant ainsi toutes les avances pour promouvoir les finances de sa maison.

- Monopole culturel.- Encore une fois on pourrait contester la qualité de vrais hamites à quelques numéros; mais la sélection de fait (opérée par hasard?) que présentent actuellement les établissements secondaires, crève les yeux. Les arguments ne manquent pas alors pour démontrer que le muhutu est inapte, qu'il est pauvre, qu'il ne sait pas se présenter. L'inaptitude est à prouver; la pauvreté est son lot dans le système social actuel; quant aux manières, une plus grande largeur d'esprit serait à souhaiter. Demain on réclamera les diplômes et ce sera juste, et les diplômes ne seront en général que d'un côté, le Muhutu ne saura même pas le sens de ce mot. Et si par hasard (la Providence nous en garde) une autre force intervenait qui sache opposer le nombre, l'aigreur et le désespoir aux diplômes! L'élément racial compliquerait tout et il n'y aura plus besoin de se poser le problème: conflit racial ou conflit social.

Nous croyons que ce monopole total est à la base des abus de tous genres dont les populations se plaignent.

Quelques faits et courants actuels peuvent faire entrevoir l'état réel d'aujourd'hui:

1) La jeunesse muhutu (quelques éléments batutsi complètement déchus ont aussi le même sort) qui a pour devise "quo itineribus semper" à l'intérieur du pays ou à l'extérieur, ayant le travail-corvée, non plus adapté à l'état et à la psychologie d'aujourd'hui, n'accepte plus ou à peine la discipline de la contrainte qui donne d'ailleurs occasion aux abus que les autorités semblent ignorer.

2) Des pères de famille qui nourrissent leur famille à peine; en politique une sorte de propagande, peut-être inconsciente, les pousse à l'antipathie à l'égard de l'Européen; bon nombre ne sont pas sans penser que le Gouvernement Belge est lié à la noblesse pour leur complète exploitation.

3) D'autre part cependant, la réflexion comme celle-ci est encore courante: "Sans l'Européen nous serions voués à une exploitation plus inhumaine qu'autrefois, à la destruction totale. C'est même malheureux que ce ne soit pas l'Européen qui devienne chef, sous-chef ou juge." Non pas qu'ils croient l'Européen parfait, mais parce que des deux maux il faut

choisir le moindre. La résistance passive à plusieurs des ordres des sous-chefs n'est que la conséquence de ce déséquilibre et de ce malaise.

4) Le regret des Bahutu de voir comment les leurs sont refoulés quasi systématiquement à des places subalternes. Toute politique employée à ce refoulement n'échappe plus qu'à quelques-uns. De tout cela, à la guerre civile "froide" et à la xénophobie il n'y a qu'un pas. De là à la popularité des idées communisantes, il n'y a qu'un pas.

**III. Propositions de solutions immédiates**

Quelques solutions peuvent être présentées et dont l'efficacité n'est possible que si le système politique et social du pays change profondément et assez rapidement.

1) La première solution est un "esprit". Qu'on abandonne la pensée que les élites ruandaises ne se trouvent que dans les rangs hamites (méthode chérie en fait par l'Administration dans nos pays et qu'on appelle par abus de terme "Umuco w'Igihugu", "le respect de la culture et de la coutume du pays").

2) Aux points de vue économique et social. Nous voulons que des institutions soient créées pour aider les efforts de la population muhutu handicapés par une administration indigène, qui semble vouloir voir le Muhutu rester dans l'indigence et donc dans l'impossibilité de réclamer l'exercice effectif de ses droits dans son pays. Nous proposons:

1° La suppression des corvées. - Les forçats seraient remplacés par un service de Travaux publics (public ou parastatal) engageant les ouvriers vraiment volontaires, qui seraient défendus par la législation sociale, dont le progrès actuel est considérable. Ce service pourrait se concevoir et se concrétiser comme la Regideso, pour autant que nous la connaissions. La suppression des corvées donnerait aux populations un minimum de liberté pour entreprendre des initiatives utiles. Des paresseux - il en est de même dans les castes d'élites - seraient surveillés par un système plus humain.

2° La reconnaissance légale de la propriété foncière individuelle dans le sens occidental du terme, chacun ayant une superficie suffisante pour culture et élevage, et les bikingi (pâturages) de la bourgeoisie seraient supprimés du moins dans le sens où la coutume les entend et les protège. Pour cette législation il faudrait qu'un service compétent détermine quelle superficie peut suffire à une famille de 6 à 8 enfants étant données les possibilités productives du sol du Ruanda-Urundi. Tous ceux qui disposeraient effectivement de cette superficie à l'heure actuelle seraient enregistrés par la sous-chefferie comme vrais propriétaires dans le sens occidental; et le reste se fera peu à peu, aidé par le mouvement de déplacement qui s'amorce dans certaines régions du pays.

Au sujet de la propriété foncière, il ne faudra pas que les mesures soient prises trop rapidement, même sur proposition du Conseil du Pays, dont bon nombre des membres seraient tentés de voir le problème d'une façon unilatérale ou sans tenir compte des difficultés ou des aspirations concrètes des roturiers de métier.

3° Un Fonds de crédit rural. - Il aurait pour but de promouvoir les initiatives rurales: agriculture rationnelle et métiers divers. Ce Fonds prêterait au manant qui veut s'établir comme agriculteur ou comme artisan. Les conditions d'accession à ce Fonds devraient cependant être telles qu'il soit abordable au Muhutu ordinaire.

4° L'union économique de l'Afrique belge et de la métropole. - Cette union devrait se faire selon des normes à préciser et à proposer d'abord au public et aux responsables avant qu'elle ne soit sanctionnée.

5° La liberté d'expression. - L'on a parlé des effets dissolvants d'une certaine Presse locale, indigène ou européenne ou même métropolitaine, tendant à diviser les races. Nous pensons quant à nous que certaines exagérations ont pu avoir lieu comme dans tout journalisme, surtout à l'âge où en sont les pays considérés. Nous croyons aussi que certaines expressions ont pu blesser certains gens non habitués à être contrariés pour faire à l'ombre ce qui leur plaît avec les petits et les faibles. Cela a pu heurter un système à peine sortant de la féodalité. Nous croyons également que devant la liberté d'expression en Afrique belge et sur les problèmes concrets concernant les populations, ne datant pas sérieusement de plus de trois ans, certaines autorités non habituées à la démocratie et qui, peut-être, ne la souhaitaient guère, se soient émotionnées. Mais nous pensons aussi qu'il ne faut pas, sous prétexte qu'il ne faut pas "diviser", taire les situations qui existent ou qui tendent à exister au préjudice d'un grand nombre et pour le monopole abusif en fait d'une minorité. Nous sommes convaincus que ce n'est pas la Justice belge ni le Gouvernement belge qui accepteraient une union réalisée sur des cadavres d'une population qui veut disposer de l'atmosphère et des conditions nécessaires pour mieux travailler et se développer. Avant de demander la perfection à la presse, ne faudrait-il pas l'exiger des tribunaux indigènes, de l'administration qui sont de loin plus importants et qui ne donnent que trop d'occasions aux critiques de la presse? La liberté bien entendue d'expression n'est-elle pas une des bases d'une vraie démocratisation? 3) Au point de vue politique. Si nous sommes d'accord que l'administration mututsi actuelle participe de plus en plus au gouvernement du pays, nous pensons pourtant mettre en garde contre une méthode qui tout en tendant à la suppression du colonialisme blanc-noir, laisserait un colonialisme pire du hamite sur le Muhutu. Il faut à la base aplanir les difficultés qui pourraient provenir du monopole hamite sur les autres races habitant, plus nombreuses et plus anciennement, dans le pays. Nous désirons à cet effet:

1° Que lois et coutumes soient codifiées. Il est certain qu'il y a certaines coutumes qu'on ne peut supprimer d'un trait de plume, mais nous croyons qu'un respect presque superstitieux du fétiche "coutume" handicape le progrès intégral et solide des populations. Aussi pour plus de clarté, d'égalité devant la loi, pour moins de confusion et d'abus, nous demandons que les lois portées par l'Autorité belge et les coutumes ayant encore vigueur utile, raisonables et non imperméables à la démocratisation du pays soient recensés en un Code qui pourrait être régulièrement revisé et modifié suivant le degré d'évolution. Les travaux déjà réalisés par les savants et les législateurs dans l'une ou l'autre matière, facilitent la rapidité d'un travail si urgent. Les tribunaux et l'administration indigènes et européens, l'essor de l'initiative privée en tout domaine ont besoin d'un tel guide. Le brandissement du glaive de la coutume du pays (umuco w'igihugu) par les intérêts monopolistes, n'est pas de nature à favoriser la confiance nécessaire, ni à établir la justice et la paix en face des aspirations actuelles de la population. Il faut recenser et codifier pour se rendre compte des déficiences réelles et les corriger pour favoriser davantage l'initiative privée qui se bute souvent aux absolutismes ou aux interprétations locales dépourvues du sens social.

2° Que soit réalisée effectivement la promotion des Bahutu aux fonctions publiques (chefferies, sous-chefferies, juges). Et concrètement nous pensons qu'il est temps que les conseils respectifs ou les contribuables élisent désormais leurs sous-chefs, chefs, leurs juges. Dans certaines localités jugées encore trop arriérées, le pouvoir pourrait proposer aux électeurs deux ou trois candidats parmi lesquels ils choisiraient leur guide.

3° Que les fonctions publiques indigènes puissent avoir une période, passée laquelle, les gens pourraient élire un autre ou réélire le sortant s'il a donné satisfaction. Un tel système, sans être raciste, donnerait plus de chances au Muhutu et ferait leçon aux abus d'un monopole à vie.

4° Le retrait des chefs de province des Conseils de chefferie.

5° La composition du Conseil du pays par les députations de chefferie: chaque chefferie déléguant un nombre proportionnel à celui de ses contribuables, sans exclure les Européens qui auraient fixé définitivement leur demeure dans la chefferie. Nous ne croyons pas simpliste d'accepter les Européens, fixés définitivement dans la circonscription; c'est, qu'établis de cette manière, ils ont des intérêts définitifs à défendre; c'est que la législation doit devenir de plus en plus élargie et moins discriminatoire, et que les Européens sont tout au moins aussi utiles qu'un Mututsi établi dans la région.

Des mesures comme celles que nous proposons nous semblent essentielles si le Gouvernement veut baser une oeuvre à avenir et sans favoritisme. Nous pouvons comprendre que l'on parle de prudence mais nous croyons que l'expérience des fameux neuf cents ans de la domination tutsi et 56 années de tutelle européenne suffit largement et qu'attendre risque de compromettre ce que l'on édifie sans ces bases.

4) Au point de vue instruction. - Demain on réclamera les diplômes et ce sera de juste. Or jusqu'ici la sélection de fait au stade secondaire et supérieur crève les yeux. Les prétextes ne manquent pas bien entendu, et certains ne sont pas dépourvus de tout fondement: ils profitent d'un système favorisant systématiquement l'avancement politique et économique du hamite.

1° Nous voulons que l'enseignement soit particulièrement surveillé. Que l'on soit plus réaliste et plus moderne en abandonnant la sélection dont on peut constater les résultats dans le secondaire. Que ce souci soit dès les premières années, de façon que l'on n'ait pas à choisir parmi presque les seuls Batutsi en cinquième année. Il n'y a peut-être pas de volonté positive de sélection, mais le fait est plus important et souvent il est provoqué par l'ensemble de ce système de remorquage dont nous parlions plus haut. Il faudra que pous éviter la sélection de fait, caeteris aequalibus, s'il n'y a pas de places suffisantes, l'on se rapporte aux mentions de livrets d'identité pour respecter les proportions. Non pas qu'il faille tomber dans le défaut contraire en bantouisant là où l'on a hamitisé. Que les positions sociales actuelles n'influencent en rien l'admission aux écoles.

2° Que l'octroi des bourses d'études (dont une bonne partie est de provenance des impôts de la population en grande partie muhutu) soit surveillé par le Gouvernement tutélaire, de façon que là non plus les Bahutu ne soient le tremplin d'un monopole qui les tienne éternellement dans une infériorité sociale et politique insupportable.

3° Quant à l'enseignement supérieur, nous pensons que les Etablissements se trouvant dans l'Afrique belge suffisent, mais qu'il faut y faire admettre le plus grand nombre possible, sans s'opposer toutefois à ce qu'il y ait des éléments - très capables qui suivent des spécialités - dans des universités métropolitaines.

Quant à l'université du Ruanda, il faudrait ne pas dilapider un budget que l'on dit déficitaire et monter d'abord l'enseignement professionnel et technique dont le Pays n'a pratiquement rien, alors que cet enseignement est à la base de l'émancipation économique. Il ne faut pas seulement obstruer systématiquement l'entrée dans les universités d'Europe à des candidats triés sur le volet et envisageant des spécialités immédiatement utiles au pays.

4° Que l'enseignement artisanal, professionnel et technique sur place soit, pour la période qui s'annonce, le premier souci du budget. Que cet enseignement soit le plus vite possible généralisé. Cet enseignement doit cependant être autant que possible à peu de frais pour permettre aux fils du peuple d'y accéder. Nous remarquons en effet que les quelques essais d'installations artisanales semblent destinés à recevoir le trop-plein de la jeunesse mututsi qui n'a pas de places ou capacités pour entrer dans le secondaire.

Nous souhaitons qu'incessamment et tant qu'on se prépare à la mise en marche de l'appareil professionnel et technique, chaque chefferie soit munie d'un centre élémentaire de formation rurale d'au moins deux ans où l'on prolonge l'enseignement primaire (appliqué à la vie) et surtout où l'on exerce un métier manuel les enfants n'accédant pas au stade secondaire. C'est pour nous, au point de vue enseignement, l'objectif principal que nous assignerions aux C.A.C. qui sont somme toute, alimentées par les impôts en grande provenance muhutu. Les crédits aux Biru (tambourineurs des Cours) et aux Danses qui recruteront normalement parmi la Noblesse, n'ont pas l'air de prouver que "c'est l'argent qui manque".

5° Que les foyers sociaux populaires soient instaurés et multipliés à l'adresse des jeunes femmes et jeunes filles du milieu rural qui, vu les finances réduites, ne peuvent accéder aux aristocratiques écoles ménagères ou de monitrices. L'équilibre de l'évolution familiale du pays exige la généralisation de cette éducation de base.

En résumé, nous voulons la promotion intégrale et collective du Muhutu; les intéressés y travaillent déjà, dans les délais que peuvent leur laisser les corvées diverses. Mais nous réclamons aussi une action d'en haut positive et plus décidée. La Belgique a fait beaucoup plus dans ce sens, il faut le reconnaître, mais il ne faut pas que son humanité s'arrête sur la route. Ce n'est pas que nous veuillions un piétinement sur place: nous sommes d'accord que le Conseil Supérieur Tutsi puisse participer progressivement et plus effectivement aux affaires du pays; mais plus fortement encore, nous réclamons du Gouvernement tutélaire et de l'Administration tutsi qu'une action plus positive en sans tergiversations soit menée pour l'émancipation économique et politique du Muhutu de la remorque hamite traditionnelle.

Dans l'ensemble, nous demandons à la Belgique de renoncer à obliger en fait le Muhutu à devoir se mettre toujours à la remorque du Mututsi. Que par exemple dans les relations sociales, on abandonne d'exiger (tacitement bien entendu) du Muhutu pour être "acceptable" de se régler sur le comportement mututsi. Puisqu'on dit respecter les cultures, il faudrait tenir compte aussi des différenciations de la culture ruandaise. Le hamite peut avoir une pratique qui plaise bien à l'un ou l'autre grand, mais nous n'avons pas encore entendu que tous les autres noirs doivent d'abord passer par une hamitisation pour pouvoir tirer de l'occidental de quoi accéder à la civilisation. Il est difficile de démontrer la nécessité de remorquer perpétuellement le muhutu au hamite, la nécessité de la médiation perpétuelle de cette remorque politique, sociale, économique, culturelle.

Les gens ne sont d'ailleurs pas sans s'être rendu compte de l'appui de l'administration indirecte au monopole tutsi. Aussi pour mieux surveiller ce monopole de race, nous nous opposons énergiquement, du moins pour le moment, à la suppression dans les pièces d'identité officielles ou privées des mentions "muhutu", "mututsi", "mutwa". Leur suppression risque encore davantage la sélection en le voilant et en empêchant la loi statistique de pouvoir établir la vérité des faits. Personne n'a dit d'ailleurs que c'est le nom qui ennuie le Muhutu; ce sont les privilèges d'un monopole favorisé, lequel risque de réduire la majorité de la population dans une infériorité systématique et une sous-existence imméritée.

C'est une volonté constructive et un sain désir de collaboration qui nous a poussés à projeter une lumière de plus sur un problème si grave devant les yeux de qui aime authentiquement ce pays; problème dans lequel les responsabilités de la tutrice Belgique ne sont que trop engagées. Ce n'est pas du tout en révolutionnaires (dans le mauvais sens du mot) mais en collaborateurs conscients de notre devoir social que nous avons tenu à mettre en garde les autorités contre les dangers que présentera sûrement tôt ou tard le maintien en fait - même simplement d'une façon négative - d'un monopole raciste sur le Ruanda. Quelques voix du peuple ont déjà signalé cette anomalie; la résistance passive, encore dans l'attente de l'intervention du Blanc tuteur, risque de s'approfondir devant les abus d'un monopole qui n'est plus accepté; qu'elle serve d'ores et déjà d'un signe.

Les autorités voudront donc voir dans cette brève note, en quelque sorte systématisés, les courants d'idées et les désirs concrets d'un peuple auquel nous appartenons, avec lequel nous partageons la vie et les refoulements opérés par une atmosphère tendant à obstruer la voie à une véritable démocratisation du pays; celle-ci, envisagée par la généreuse Belgique est vivement souhaitée par la population avide d'une atmosphère politico-sociale viable et favorable à l'initiative et au travail pour un mieux-être et pour la promotion intégrale et collective du peuple.

Maximilien NIYONZIMA
Godefroid SENTAMA
Grégoire KAYBANDA
Silvestre MUNYAMBONERA
Claver NDAHAYO
Joseph SIBOMANA
Isidore NZEYIMANA
Joseph HABYARIMANA
Calliopé MULINDAHABI

**NOTES:**